MAKING OUT IN KOREAN

MAKING OUT
IN
KOREAN

Peter Constantine

I would like to thank June Kim for his assistance in compiling and checking the examples and information in this book. I am also especially grateful to Chris Baek and Sue Lee for their knowledgeable help. Robert Muldrow and Sunny Teichmann also made an important contribution.

Illustrations by Philippe Schmidt.

YENBOOKS
2-6, Suido 1-chome, Bunkyo-ku, Tokyo 112, Japan
©1995 by YENBOOKS

ISBN 4-900737-33-X
LCC Card No. 94-61452

First edition, 1995
Third reprinting,1998

Printed in Singapore

CONTENTS

INTRODUCTION

Making Out in Korean is your guide to the living language. It will help you successfully navigate your way through the colorful Korean social scene. In 13 easy chapters you can learn how to meet people, make friends, and dine out. With the phrases in this book, you'll be able to hold your own anywhere, from bustling train stations and crowded provincial markets to Seoul's fast-paced restaurant, bar, and club world.

No grammar drills! No complicated language rules! No long word lists! *Making Out in Korean* avoids the flamboyant linguistics of the highly formal language taught in schools and universities, offering instead the plain and candid language of the average person on the street.

Whether you trek through South Korea or venture onto the unbeaten paths of North Korea— *Making Out in Korean* will give you the words you need for polite conversation, intimate encounters, and even rough-and-tumble situations should such occasions arise.

INFORMATION

Making Out in Korean taps into the new, spontaneous, vocal language spoken by Korea's Generation X: the debonair teenagers, the fast-moving downtown clubsters, and partying post-yuppies. Westerners who have tried to wrestle their way through Korean courses will be relieved to discover this simpler, more relaxed version of the language, in which formal syntax, elaborate vocabulary, tongue-twisting sounds, and cumbersome morphological patterns are often thrown to the wind in favor of quicker, more natural turns of phrase.

The spoken language is changing fast, and Korean elders often goggle in confusion when the modish crowd speaks. For example, whereas an uptight member of the older generation would approach you with the phrase *Sonseng-in chesong hamnida,* "Oh, excuse me, sir," a hip, young Seoulite might simply exclaim *Ya imma,* "Yo! Dude!" The grammatically correct but staid *Anyong hashimnika,* "How do you do?" becomes the friendlier *Chal itsoso,* "How you doin'?"

The new approach to polite speech is even more radical. One of the biggest hurdles in formal Korean, Westerners often complain, is its intricate system of levels of diction, where age, sex, and the social standing of the speakers determine the grammar and words to be used. Not so with Generation X! As you will see in *Making Out in Korean,* trendy speakers prefer a brasher approach. The highly formal and polite verb endings, for instance, are often the first things to go. In punctilious Korean, "I want" is *wonhamnida.* The next step down in formality is the polite *wonhe yo,* and the most casual is *wonhe.*

VERB BASICS

In Korean, verbs are usually placed at the end of a phrase or sentence. One salient feature of Korean verbs is that they express neither person nor tense. *Wonhe,* for instance, can mean I, you, he, she, it, we, or they want/s, is/are wanting, will want.

Pronouns (I, you, he, she, we, it, and they) are unnecessary in Korean, unless what you are saying is unclear, or you wish to be specifically emphatic.

In the first four examples below, pronouns are omitted because they can be inferred from their contexts—a statement is obviously about "me," while a question concerns "you." The pronoun in the fifth example would be unnecessary if it weren't delivering emphasis.

I'm going to Seoul.   *So-ul e kalkoya.*
(Seoul to go)

You going to Seoul?   *So-ul e kalkoya?*
(Seoul to go)

I want that. (that want)	*Chogo wonhe.*
Do you want that? (that want)	*Chogo wonhe?*
I want that! (I that want)	*Na chogo wonhe!*

Since Korean verbs have no tenses, the future tense can be expresed through use of words such as *kot,* "soon," *itaga,* "later," *ne-il,* "tomorrow," and *taum chu,* "next week."

I'll be going to Seoul soon.	*So-ul e kot kalkoya.*
Will you be going to Seoul later?	*So-ul e itaga kalkoya?*
I'll be going to Seoul tomorrow.	*Ne-il so-ul e kalkoya.*

There are various ways of forming negative sentences. The simplest way is to add the prefix *an,* "not."

I don't want that.	*Chogo an-wonhe.*
I'm not going to Seoul.	*So-ul e an-kalkoya.*

PRONUNCIATION

After your new Korean friends overcome their initial surprise at hearing you, a foreigner, speak Korean, the ice will be broken and communicating will be fun. The transliteration of Korean in this book is a simplified version of the official system of romanization and is more suited to recreating the casual vernacular. Still, the Korean language does have sounds not found in English. Your best guideline is to listen to the people you meet and imitate their speech.

Vowels

a	as in car
e	as in pen
i	as in it
o	as in raw
u	as in soon

Consonants

ch You will find that young speakers in Seoul often pronounce ch so that it sounds almost like j as in jet. The official transliteration tries to render closely related sounds as "ch'," "j," and "jj." For simplicity, however, *Making Out in Korean* uses only *ch.*

d as in dog

g as in goat

k as in king, often pronounced almost as a g

> *p* as in put, often pronounced almost as a b
> *r* pronounced almost as an l
> *s* as in small
> *sh* as in ship
> *t* as in tap, often pronounced almost as a d

NOTE: In examples where more than one Korean translation is provided, the phrases are listed in descending order of politeness.

WHAT'S UP?

VERY POLITE GREETINGS

How are you? | *Anyong hashimnika?*
Anyong haseyo?*

> * These two expressions are the most polite Korean greetings and can be used at any time of the day or night. Literally, they mean "Are you at peace?" A typical response might be either of the following two phrases.

I've been fine. | *Ne, chal chinetsoyo.**

I'm fine. | *Chal chineyo.†*

> * Literally, "Yes, it was well spent."
> † Literally, "Well spent."

How do you do? | *Otoke chineseyo?*
Oteyo?

What's new? | *Pyol-il opchiyo?*
Pyol-il opsuseyo?

Nothing much.	*Kucho kureyo.*
Things are hard.	*Himduroyo.*
Things are busy.	*Yochum bapoyo.*
How have you been?	*Chal chine shotsoyo?*
I've been fine, thank you.	*Chal chinetsoyo.*

VERY CASUAL GREETINGS

How you doin'?	*Chal itsoso?*
Yo, what's up?	*Imma, chal itsonni?*
Dude, what's up?	*Sekiya, chal itsonni?** *Chashiga, chal itsonni?**

* *Seki,* "baby animal," and *chashi,* "human baby," are used in Korean slang the way "asshole" is used in American English. When said to one's closest friends, they can be warm, bonding expressions—but handle with care.

How you been?	*Otoke chinetni?*
Dude, how you been?	*Sekiya, otoke chinetni?* *Chashiga, otoke chinetni?*

| I'm fine! | *Chal itsoso!* |
| | *Chal chinetso!* |

| Have you been doin' OK? | *Chal chinetni?* |

Yeah, man!	*Kure,* ichashiga!*
	Kure, imma!
	Kure, isekiya!

* This casual word for "yes," and the even more casual *ung* and *uhuh,* are often used among friends as answers to "What's up?"

| Where did you go to? | *Odi katsoso?* |

It's been a while.	*Oren-maniya.*
Yeah!	*Kure!* *Uhuh!* *Ung!*
Yeah, it's been ages.	*Kure, oren-maniya.* *Ung, oren-maniya.*
Have you been around?	*Chibe itsoso?*
How's Peter/Mary?	Peter/Mary *chal chinetni?* Peter/Mary *chal itchi?* Peter/Mary *chal itni?*
Peter/Mary is fine.	Peter/Mary *chal chine.* Peter/Mary *chal iso.*
How are Peter and Mary?	Peter *wa* Mary *chal chinetni?*
Peter and Mary are fine.	Peter *wa* Mary *chal iso.*
Anything new with Peter/Mary?	Peter/Mary *pyol-il omni?* Peter/Mary *pyol-il opchi?*
He/She's doing fine.	*Pyol-il opso.*

They're doing fine.
He/She is OK.

Chal chine.

He/She's doing so-so.

Ke kucho kure.
Kucho kure.

What's wrong, man?

We kure, imma?

Nothing's wrong with me.

Amu koto aniya.

What are you doing here?

Ochon iriya?
Yogi we watso?

Nothing special.

Kunyang watso.

None of your business.

Namiya.*

> * Literally, "Other person." The idea is: "That is the
> kind of question you could ask yourself, but I'm
> another person, not you—so none of your business!"

Mind your own business.	*Chamgyon hachima.*
	Sang-guan ma.
Go away!	*Kocho!*
Go away, man!	*Kocho, imma!*
Fuck off!	*Chokka!**

> * Literally, "Kick penis!" From *chot*, "penis," and *ka*, "kick."

Really?	*Chongmal?*
	Chongmalo?
	Chongmaliya?
Are you serious?	*Chincha?*
	Chincharo?
	Chinchaya?
Oh, yeah?	*Kure?*
You're lying!	*Kochimal!*
Are you lying?	*Kochimal ichi?*
Don't lie!	*Kochimal ma!*
Stop lying!	*Kochimal hachima!*
What?	*Muo?*
	Mo?

Huh?	*Ung?*
I don't believe it!	*Anmido!*
	Midulsu opso!
Why?	*We?*
Why not?	*We aniya?*
	We ande?
You're joking!	*Nongdam ichi!*
You're not joking?	*Nongdam anichi?*
I'm not joking.	*Nongdam aniya.*
He's joking!	*Nongdam igetchi!*

Are you making fun of me? *Nolinun goya?*

I guess so. *Kuroketchi.*

Maybe. *Ochomyon.*

Maybe not. *Anilkoya.*

That's impossible. *Mot halkoya.*
Halsu opso.

You can't do that. *Hachimote.*

I don't care. *Nan sanguan opso.*

It's got nothing to do
with me. *Narang sanguan opso.*

I'm not interested.	*Sengkak opso.*
I think that is it.	*Chogo ga-te.*
I think this is it.	*Igo ga-te.*
You're crazy!	*No michotso!*
Damn!	*Ai shibal!* *Ai shippal!*
That's right.	*Macho.*
Is this it?	*Igoya?*
This is it.	*Igoya.*

Sure.	*Kurom.*
It's true.	*Kuge macho.*
I understand.	*Araturoso.*
No problem.	*Munche opso.*
I like it!	*Choatso!*
Me, too.	*Na do.*
	Na du.
OK!	*Aratso!**

* Literally, "I know."

Yo!	*Ya!*
	Imma!
Great!	*Choa!**

* Literally, "I like it."

I hope so.	*Kure-yachi.*
It's risky.	*Wihom-he.*
Cheer up. (Smile)	*Uso.*

BASICS

Yes.	*Ne.*
Yeah.	*Uh.*
No.	*Aniyo.*
	Ani.
Right.	*Kure.*
What?	*Mo?*
	Muo?
Who?	*Nugu?*

Where?	*Odi?*
When?	*Onche?*
Why?	*We?*
How?	*Otoke?*
Whose?	*Nugukoya?*
This.	*Igo.*
That.	*Chogo.*
Here.	*Yogi.*
There.	*Chogi.*
Maybe.	*Ama.*
Maybe not.	*Ama anilkoya.*
I	*Na*
You	*No*
He/She	*Che* (used in person's presence) *Ke* (used in person's absence)

We	*Uri*
You (plural)	*No-nedul*
They	*Che-nedul*
Don't!	*Hachima!*
Please.	*Chebal.*
Thank you.	*Kamsamnida.*
Can I have that?	*Igo kachodo teyo?*
How much is this?	*Igo olma eyo?*
That's so cheap.	*Igo we iroke sayo.*
That's not cheap.	*Sange ani eyo.*
That's too expensive!	*Nomu pisayo!*
I'm not buying that.	*Igo ansalkeyo.*
Make it cheaper and I'll buy it.	*Chomto samyonun salkeyo.*

GOT A MINUTE?

One moment.	*Chamkan man kidalyo.* *Chamkan man.*
When?	*Onche?*
'Til when?	*Onche kachi?*
What time?	*Myoshiye?*
Am I too early?	*Na nomu ilchik watchi?*

Is it too late?	*Nomu nuchotchi?*
When is it good for you?	*Oncheka choa?*
What time is good for you?	*Myoshika choa?*
How about later?	*Itakan ote?*
How about tomorrow?	*Ne-il un ote?*
How about the day after tomorrow?	*More nun ote?*
When can I come?	*Na onche kalsu itso?*
When can we go?	*Uri onche chum kalsu itso?*
What time do we arrive?	*Uri onche chum dochak-he?*
What time will we be back?	*Uri onche chum dorawa?*
Are you ready?	*Chunbi tetso?*
When will you do it?	*Onche halkoya?*
When will you be done?	*Onche kunalsu itso?*

How long will it take?	*Olma-kum kol-yo?*
It'll be done soon.	*Kumbang telkoya.*
Not now.	*Chikum ande.*
Before.	*Kuchone.*
Next time.	*Ta-ume.*
I don't know.	*Mola.*
I don't know when.	*Onche telchi mola.*
I don't know now.	*Chikum-un mola.*
I'm not sure.	*Huakshil-hi mola.*
	Huakshilin mola.
Sometime (later).	*Itaga.*
Any time's OK.	*Amutena choa.*
	Onche rado choa.
Everyday.	*Men-nal.*
You decide when.	*Niga onchenchi kyolchong-he.*
Whenever you want.	*Niga wonha-nun tero-he.*

OK, let's meet then.   *Kurom, kute man-na.*

Let's go!   *Kacha!*

Let's go for it.   *Bali shichak hacha.**

    * Literally, "Let's start fast."

Hurry up.   *Bali.*

Let's start again.   *Tashi shichakacha.*

Let's continue.   *Kesok hacha.*

Let's do it later.   *Itaga hacha.*

Yeah!   *Kurom!*
                            Acha!

I'll do it quickly.	*Bali halke.*
I'll finish soon.	*Kumbang kutnalkoya.*
I finished.	*Kutnatso.*
Finished?	*Kutnatso?*

HEY THERE!

Listen to what I'm saying!   *Ne malchom turopa!*

Listen to him/her.   *Che malchom turopa.*

Listen to them.   *Che-nedul malchom turopa.*

Did you hear me?   *Ne mal turotso?*

Can you hear me?   *Ne mal tur-lyo?**

    * Literally, "Can you hear my voice clearly?"

Do you understand?   *Aratso?*

Do you understand, or not?   *Aratso, molatso?*

Can you understand me?   *Ne mal ihe-he?*

I don't understand.   *Na ihe mote.*

I didn't understand.   *Na ihe moteso.*

I couldn't understand.   *Na ihe halsu opsotso.*

What?   *Morago?*

What did you say?   *Morago malhetso?*

I don't understand what   *Monsorinchi ihe mote.*
    you're saying.

Don't say such things.   *Kuron mal hachima.*

You shouldn't say things   *Kurumal hamyon ande.*
    like that.

Did you say that?   *Niga kumal hetso?*

You said that, right?   *Niga kumal han-ge
                               matchi?*

I didn't say that.	*Nega kumal hanchok opso.*
I didn't say anything.	*Nan amumaldo anhetso.*
I didn't tell anyone.	*Nugu egedo malhachi anatso.*
Let's speak Korean!	*Hanguk malo hacha!**

* Literally, "Let's do it in Korean."

Can you speak Korean?	*Hanguk mal halsu isuseyo?** *Hanguk mal halsu itso?*

* An *extremely* polite way of asking.

Let's talk!	*Yegi hacha!*
Let's talk more.	*Chogumdo yegi-he.*
Let's talk later.	*Itaga yegihe.*
Tell me later.	*Kuyegi nachung-e.*
I don't wanna talk.	*Yegi hago shipchi ana.*
I don't wanna talk with you.	*Norang yegi hago shipchi ana.*
I don't wanna hear about it.	*Kumal dudko shipchi ana.*
I don't wanna hear about that thing.	*Kuyegi dutko shipchi ana.*
Don't make excuses!	*Pyonmyong hachima!*
Don't give me no excuses!	*Nege kuron pinge techima!*
Stop complaining.	*Chansori hachima.*
Don't talk so loud.	*Kuge mal hachima.*
Speak up.	*Kuge malhe.*

Speak louder.   *To kuge malhe.*

Say it again.   *Tashi malheba.*

LOOK AT THAT!

5

Look!	*Yogiba!*
Look at this!	*Igo chomba!*
Look at that!	*Chogo chomba!*
Don't look!	*Pochima!*
Don't look at this/that.	*Igo/Chogo pochima.*
Can you see it?	*Igo polsu itso?*
Did you see that?	*Chogo patso?*
I see it clearly.	*Chalpoyo.*
I saw it.	*Chogo patso.*
Did you see it?	*Igo patso?*
I can't see it.	*Polsu opso.*
I didn't see it.	*Mot patso.*

I don't see it.	*Anboyo.*
I don't wanna see it.	*Bogi shiro.*
Did you see Kim?	*Kim patso?*
I wanna see you soon.	*No bali pogoshipo.*
I'm gonna meet Kim soon.	*Kim kot polkoya.*
Are you gonna meet Kim soon?	*Kim kot polkoya?*
Did you meet John?	*John man-na sotso?*
I met John.	*John man-na sotso.*
Well, we meet again.	*Dotashi manane.*

COMING AND GOING

6

Come here!   *Yogi wa!*

Come over here!   *Yogiro wa!*

Come later.   *Nachung-e wa.*

Can you come?   *Olsu itso?*
      Olsu itni?

Come with me.   *Nawa kachiga.*

He/She's coming here.	*Ke yogi olkoya.*
They are coming here.	*Ke-nedul yogi olkoya.*
I'll go soon.	*Na kot kalke.*
I'll come over soon.	*Na kot nolo kalke.*
I can go.	*Kalsu itso.*
I think I can go.	*Kalsu itsulko kat-he.*
I can't go.	*Kalsu opso.* *Motka.*
I wanna go.	*Na kagoshipo.*
Do you wanna go?	*No kagoshipo?*
Do they wanna go?	*Ke-nedul kagoshipo he?*
I wanna go to Seoul.	*Na so-ul kagoshipo.*
I really wanna go.	*Na chongmal kagoshipo.*
I don't wanna go.	*Na kagoshipchi ana.*
I really don't wanna go.	*Na chongmal kagoshipchi ana.*

You're going, right?	*No kanun kochi?*
I'm going.	*Na kalkoya.*
I'm not going.	*Na ankalkoya.*
I didn't go.	*Na ankatsoso.*
	Na ankatso.
Don't go!	*Kachima!*
Don't go yet!	*Achik kachima!*
I have to go.	*Na chigum kayade.*

I must go now.	*Na chigum gok kayade.*
May I go?	*Na kadode?*
I'm going. I'm leaving.	*Na kanda.*
Shall we go?	*Uri kalka?*
Let's go!	*Kacha!*
Let's get outa here!	*Nagacha!*
Let's split!	*Hut-to chicha!* *Chicho chicha!**

* Literally, "Let's rip it."

He/She left. ·   *Che donatso.*

Stay here!   *Yogi itso!*

Where are you going?   *No odiga?*

Go slowly.   *Chonchonhi ka.*

FOOD

I'm hungry. *Na pekopa.*

I'm starving. *Na pekopaso michiketso.**

> * Literally, "I'm going crazy from hunger."

Have you eaten? *No bulso mogotni? Bulso mogotni?*

I haven't eaten yet. *Na achik anmogoso. Achik anmogoso.*

Do you wanna eat something? *No mo mokoshipo? Mo mokoshipo?*

I'd like to eat something. *Na mo mokoshipo. Mo mokoshipo.*

Do you want some more? *To mokoshipo? To mokul-le?*

I'm thirsty. *Na mokmalyo. Mokmalyo.*

I wanna drink some beer.	*Na mekchu mashile.*
	Mekchu mashile.
I want some liquor.	*Na sul mashile.*
	Sul mashile.
Try some _____.	*_____ masho.**

> * *Masho* literally means "liquid." "Try some" is implied.

Korean vodka	*Soju*
Strong, milky rice liquor	*Makoli*
This tastes too weird.	*Igo mashi isang-he.*
I think this has gone bad.	*Igo sang-hetso.*
I think this stuff's stale.	*Igo mashi katso.**

> * Literally, "This taste has left."

Wow! This tastes good!	*Wa! Mashita!*
More, more!	*Tocho, tocho!*
	To, to!
Would you like to drink some more?	*To mashile?*

Thank you, but I still have plenty.	*Komapchiman achik mani namasoyo.* *Komapchiman achik mani namaso.*
Come on, dude, have some more!	*Kurochi malgo domasho, imma!*
It's on me!	*Nega nelke!**
* Literally, "I'll pay!"	
How about some food?	*Pap mokoshipo?*
Is the food ready?	*Pap chunbi teso?* *Pap ta teso?*
Yeah, it's ready.	*Ta chunbi teso.* *Ta teso.*

This is a feast!   *Chinsu songchan ieyo!**

> * A formula phrase used when one is invited for dinner.

Try this!   *Igo mogoba!*

Try that!   *Chogo mogoba!*

Dude, stuff your face!   *Imma, pali chomogo!*

That looks delicious.   *Nomu mashike poyo.*

Wow, it looks delicious!   *Wa, mashiketa!*

Oh, that smells good!   *Aa, nemse choa!*

What's this?   *Igo moya?*

Taste it.   *Matchomba.*

What's it called?	*Igo morago pulo?*
Is it hot? (spicy)	*Igo mewo?*
This is boiling!	*Atugo!*
Yuck!	*Uuah!*
It tastes like shit!	*Mashi dong kat-he!*
It's awful!	*Mat opso!*
I can't eat this!	*Igo mot mogo!*
Water, water!	*Mul, mul!*
My tongue's on fire!	*Na ibeso pul-na!*
How d'you eat this?	*Igo otoke mognun koyeyo?* *Igo otoke mogo?*
Are those chopsticks?	*Igo chotgarak iya?*
Give me a fork.	*Na poku cho.*
You want a knife?	*Kal chulga?*
Please try this *sunde*.* It tastes good.	*Sunde chom mogoba.*

* A Korean dish made of stuffed pig intestines.

Have some *bondegi!**   *Bondegi mogoba!*

> * Another exotic Korean specialty, made from boiled cocoons.

I'd like to try some   *Na poshingtang*
   *poshingtang.**   mokoshipo.*

> * Steamed dog-meat stew.

Careful, that *tokpoki** is   *Choshime, tokpoki*
   hot!   *mewo!*

> * *Ultra*-spicy red bean paste.

That's a dip, don't drink it!   *Chigo mongnun koya,*
    mashichima!

Give me some.   *Na chom cho.*

Give me a little more.   *Chogum to cho.*

I'd like more food.   *Na to mogule.*

You want more food?   *No to mogule?*

Enough?   *Tetso?*

Enough!   *Tetso!*

I LIKE IT!

I like this.

Na igo choa.
Igo choa.

I like that.

Na kugo choa.
Chogo choa.

I really like that!

*Na chogo chongmal
choa!*

I don't like that.

Na kugo shiro.
Na chogo shiro.

I don't really like it.

*Na igo kuroke choa
hachi ana.*

No, thanks.*

Kuenchan ayo.
Tetsoyo.
Kuenchana.
Tetso.

* An abrupt "No, thank you" can sound very rude.
Kuenchan ayo and its more casual version *kuenchana*
literally mean "It is OK," while *tetsoyo* and the casual
tetso mean "It is done."

I want _____.	*Na _____ won-he.*
this	*igo*
that	*chogo*
I want _____. (use with nouns)	*Na _____ katkoshipo.*
I don't want _____.	*Na _____ katki shiro.*
a computer	*kompyuta*
a camera	*kamera*

a radio	*radio*
a video recorder	*pidio*
a tape	*kasetu*
a TV	*tibi*

I don't need that.	*Na chogo piryo opso.*
	Na kugo piryo opso.
I don't need this.	*Na igo piryo opso.*
I'm busy.	*Na papo.*
I'm happy.	*Na kipo.*
I'm glad to know that.	*Na kugo turoso kipo.*
I'm sad.	*Na sulpo.*
	Na u-ulhe.
I'm fine.	*Na kuenchana.*
I'm afraid.	*Na musowo.*

I'm getting sick of it.   *Na shilchung na.*

I'm irritated!   *Chachung na!*

Man, I'm irritated!   *Ai, chachung na!*

I'm confused!   *Moga monchi mola!**

> * Literally, "I don't know which is which."

I'm going crazy.   *Na michigetso.*

I'm pissed off.   *Na pichotso.*

I'm mad! (angry)   *Na huanatso!*

I'm ready.   *Na chunbi detso.*

I'm sleepy.   *Na cholyo.*

I'm tired.   *Na pigonhe.*

I'm wasted.   *Na katso.**

   * Literally, "I left!" Too much alcohol, too many
   parties. . .

I'm totally wasted!   *Na chongmal katso!*

I'm out of it!   *Na ping gatso!**

   * My head is going "ping!"—i.e., it's spinning.

I'm bored!   *Tabunhe!*
                              Chiruhe!

I feel sick.   *Na apo.*

I'm disappointed.   *Na shilmang hetso.*

I'm disappointed in you.   *Na nohante shilmang
                              hetso.*

What a drag!   *Aa, tabunhe!*
                              Aa, chiruhe!

Oh, God! (How awful!)   *Hananim mapsosa!*

What a pity!   *Namu amitabul!*

Can you do it?   *Halsu itso?*

I can do it.   *Halsu itso.*

I can't do it.	*Halsu opso.*
Sorry, I can't do it.	*Halsu opsoso, mianhe.*
Sorry.	*Che song hamnida.** *Mianhe.*

* An extremely polite apology.

I can't believe it.	*Midul suga opso.*
I'll do it.	*Nega halke.*
I know.	*Aratso.*
I know him/her.	*Na che aro.* (used in person's presence) *Na ke aro.* (used in person's absence)
Do you know that?	*No kugo aro?* *No chogo aro?*
Oh, you know that.	*No kugo alchana.*
I don't know.	*Na mola.*

I'll think about it.	*Chom sengake polke.*
I'm so confused.	*Nomu hekal-lyo.*
I made a mistake.	*Nega shilsu hetso.*
Am I right?	*Nega macho?*
Am I wrong?	*Nega tulyo?*

FIGHTING

What do you want?	*Moya?*
What do you want, asshole?	*Moya, imma?* *Moya, ichashiga?* *Moya, ishekiya?*
What?	*Mo?*
What you lookin' at?	*Molpa?*
Anything wrong?	*Munche itso?*
You givin' me attitude?	*We cheryoba?**

* Literally, "Why are you looking down at me?"

What are you staring at?	*Mol chodaba?*
Excuse me? What did you just say?	*Morago?*
Do you know who I am?	*Nega nugunchi aro?*
Come here, I'll teach you some manners!	*Sakachi omnun shekya, iluwa!**

    * Literally, "You have no manners, baby. Come here!"

Come here!	*Iluwa!*
Don't joke with me!	*Narang nongdam hachima!*
Don't mess around with me!	*Narang changnan hachima!*
Stop it!	*Hachima!*
Shut up!	*Iptakcho!*
What're you doing?	*Mo hanen chishiya?*
What'd you hit me for?	*We cho?*
What'd you push me for?	*We miro?*

I'm gonna kill you!	*No chugyo porilkoya!*
Have you finished?	*Takunatso?*
You wanna fight?	*Saule?*
We gonna fight, or not?	*Saulkoya, malkoya?*
Let's fight and see!	*Monjo saoba!*
Ouch!	*Aa!*
Don't!	*Kuman!*
That hurts!	*Apo!*
Help!	*Toachuseyo!*
	*Saram salyo!**

* Literally, "Save a person's life!"

Don't hit me!	*Kuman teryo!*
You deserve it!	*Machul chisul hetso!*
Don't do it again!	*Tashi hachima!*
Say you're sorry!	*Miyan hatago-he!*
Sorry.	*Miyan-he.*
You're right.	*Niga macho.*
I was wrong.	*Nega tulyoso.*
It was my fault.	*Nega chalmoteso.*
Forgive me.	*Yongso hecho.*
I forgive you.	*Yongso hechulke.*
You're making me laugh!	*Utkine!*
You win.	*Niga igyaso.*
I lose.	*Nega chotso.*

SPECIAL KOREAN INSULTS

I'll kick your penis!	*Chokka!*

You are lower than an insect.	*Polemando motan chashik.*
Son of a beggar.	*Kuchi seki.*
Son of a retard.	*Pyongshin seki.*
Son of an idiot.	*Pabo seki.*
Son of a whore.	*Ship seki.*
Prostitute!	*Shipal!**

* Literally, "Eighteen." A pun on *ship,* "body," and *pal,* "sale." A gender-neutral term.

Gigolo!	*Shipalom!**

* Literally, "Eighteen men." A pun on *ship,* "body," and *palom,* "seller."

Whore!	*Shipalyon!**

* Literally, "Eighteen women."

You peasant!	*Sangyon!* (women) *Sangnom!* (men)
You look like a penis!	*Chokatunom!* (men) *Chokatunyon!* (women)

Don't show off!	*Chalan chok hachima!*
Go drink your mother's breast milk and then come back!	*Kaso omma choshina tomoko wa!*
Go home and masturbate!	*Chibena kaso taltal-i cho!*
Are you insane?	*Wenchiral? No michoso?*
Crazy man!	*Michinom!*
Crazy woman!	*Michinyon!*
Ah, stupid!	*Aa, mushik!*
Stonehead!	*Tolmori!*
Pig!	*Duechi!*

Turnip-legs!   *Mudari!**

     * Said of women with fat legs.

Short-legs!   *Shotari!**

     * From English "short" and the Korean *tari,* "legs."

Fatty!   *Dungbo!*

Look at that meat fat!   *Cho pigesal chomba!**

     * Used as a taunt for obese individuals.

Hippopotamus!   *Hama!*

Bad-luck-woman!   *Mang halyon!*

Oh, I lost my appetite!*   *Aa, pamadopso!*

     * Implies that the person being insulted is so
     unseemly that the speaker's stomach is turning.

Pervert!   *Chochil!*

You are a dirty man.   *Turo-unom.*

You are a dirty woman.   *Turo-unyon.*

Oh, shit smell!   *Aa, dong nemsena!*

Die!	*Chugo!*
Why don't you go somewhere and die!	*Odi kaso chugo poryo!*
Son of a white man!*	*Peginseki!*

* An insult used to taunt Westerners. Other politically incorrect expressions are: *gomshi,* "Sir Black," for people of African descent; *chanke,* a type of Chinese-Korean dish, for Chinese; and, *ilbonseki,* "Son of Japan," for Japanese.

PARTY TALK

10

Do you come here often? *Yogi chachu wayo?*

You look like you're having fun. *Cham chemiso boineyo.*

Yes, I'm having fun. *Ne, chulgigo isoyo.*

This place is happening! *Yogi kuenchancho!*

Yeah, this place is happening! *Yogi kuenchanayo!*

This place is fun.	*Yogi chongmal chemisoyo.*
This place is fantastic.	*Yogi moshisoyo.*
What's your name?	*Irumi otoke teseyo?*
My name is _____.	*Ne irumun _____ imnida.*
Are you here alone?	*Honcha oshosoyo?*
Yes, I'm here alone.	*Honcha watsoyo.*
No, I'm here with my _____.	*Aniyo, _____ rang watsoyo.*
father	*apa*
mother	*omma*

friends	*chingu*
boyfriend	*namchachingu*
girlfriend	*yochachingu*
husband	*nampyon*
wife	*ane*
Can I join you?	*Kachi itsodo teyo?*
Can I sit here?	*Yogi anchodu teyo?*
Is someone sitting here?	*Yogi nugu anchasoyo?*
Someone's sitting here.	*Yogi nuga anchasoyo.*
Please sit down.	*Ye, anchuseyo.*
Can I buy you a drink?	*Sulsado deyo?*
Where are you from?	*Odiso oshotsoyo?*
I'm from ____.	*Na ____ eso watsoyo.*
the U.S.	*miguk*
England	*yonguk*

France	*purangsu*
Australia	*osuturelia*
Germany	*togil*
Japan	*ilbon*
I live in _____.	*Na _____ eso sarayo.*
New York	*nyu yok*
L.A.	*elei*

Seoul	*so-ul*
How old are you?	*Naiga otoke teyo?*
I am _____ years old.	_____ *sal iyeyo.*
15	*Yol taso*
16	*Yol yoso*
17	*Yol il gop*
18	*Yol yoder*
19	*Yol ahop*
20	*Sumul*
21	*Sumul han*
22	*Sumul tu*
23	*Sumul se*
24	*Sumul ne*

25	*Sumul taso*
30	*Sorun*
31	*Sorun han*
40	*Mahun*
41	*Mahun han*
50	*Shihun*
60	*Yesun*
70	*Irun*
80	*Ahun*
90	*Nahun*
Are you a student?	*Hakseng iseyo?*
Where do you work?	*Odiso ilhaseyo?*
I'm a _____.	*Na _____ eyo.*
doctor	*usa*
dentist	*chikua-usa*
lawyer	*pyonhosa*

secretary	*piso*
pilot	*chochongsa*

driver	*unchonsa*
Wow, what a nice job you've got!	*O, moshinun ilhashineyo!*
What kinds of hobbies do you have?	*Oton chimil kako keseyo?*
I like _____.	*Nan _____ chowa heyo.*
sports	*undong ul*
tennis	*tenisu rul*

golf	*kolpu rul*
music	*uma gul*
ballet	*pale rul*
What music do you like?	*Oton uma gul choa haseyo?*
You know this song?	*I nore aseyo?*
Yes, I do.	*Ne, arayo.*
I don't know it.	*Moru ketsoyo.*
This is the first time I'm hearing it.	*Choum tunun deyo.*

Would you like to dance? — *Chum chushileyo?*

I can't dance. — *Na chum motchoyo.*

I'm not in the mood. — *Chum chul kibuni aniyeyo.*

You dance well. — *Chum chal chushinunteyo.*

Shall we go elsewhere? — *Odi tandero kacho?*

Where shall we go? — *Odiro kalkayo?*

What time do you have to be home? — *Chibe myoshikachi kayadeyo?*

What time are you leaving? — *Myoshiye kashilkoyeyo?*

Don't go yet. — *Chigum kachimaseyo.*

Go later! — *Itaga kayo!*

What shall we do? — *Mo haleyo?*

What's next? — *Tamun moyeyo?*

It's up to you. — *Hago shipun dero haseyo.*

Do you wanna come to my place?

Uri chiburo kaleyo?

I'm not sure.

Chal moru ketsoyo.

Just for coffee.

Kunyang kopi mashiro kayo.

Yes, let's go.

Ne, kacho.

GETTING SERIOUS

I want to know more about you.	*No-e teheso to algoshipo.*
Shall we meet again?	*Uri to manale?*
When can I see you again?	*Onche tashi manalsu itni?* *Onche nolpolsu itni?*
Can I call you?	*Nega chonwa hedode?*
Here's my phone number.	*Ige ne chonwa ponoya.*
What's your number?	*No chonwa ponhoka otoke te?*
Will you call me?	*Nante chonwa hechulsu itni?*
It was fun.	*Chemi itsoso.*

ON THE PHONE

Hello.	*Yoboseyo.*

Hello.	*Anyong haseyo.*
This is Robert. Is Mary at home?	*Cho* Robert *indeyo,* Mary *chibe isoyo?*
Mary is out.	Mary *odi naganunde.*
Wait a minute.	*Chamkaman kidalyopa.*
Mary! Telephone!	Mary-*ya! Chonwa pado!*
It's me, Robert.	*Na* Robert *iya.*
What are you doing?	*Chigum mohe?*
Shall we meet now?	*Chigum man-nale?*
I wanna see you.	*No pogoshipo.*
I can't go out now.	*Chigum nagalsu opso.*

I'll call you tomorrow.	*Nega ne-il chonwa halke.*
Bye!	*Chal itso!** *Chalga!†*

* Literally, "Stay well." Usually said by the person who called.

† Literally, "Go well." Said by the person who was called.

LOVERS' LANGUAGE

I love you.	*Sarang-he.*
I'm crazy about you.	*No-hante michigetso.*
I'm yours.	*Nan nikoya.*
You're mine.	*Non nekoya.*
You are beautiful.	*No yepo.*
You are handsome.	*No chal sengyoso.*

You're sexy.	*No yahe.*
Your _____ is/are beautiful.	*No _____ yepo.*
eyes	*nuni*
lips	*ipsuri*
hands	*soni*
face	*olguri*
teeth	*ipari*
legs	*tariga*
nose	*koga*
breasts	*choshi*
neck	*mogi*
You have a beautiful body.	*No yepun momerul kachigo iso.*
You smell nice.	*No nemseka choa.*
Can I kiss you?	*Nega popo hedote?*
Kiss me!	*Popo hecho!*

Do you wanna sleep with me?	*Narang kachi chagoshipo?*
Oh, I'm embarrassed.	*Ai, chengpi-he.*
Don't be shy.	*Suchupum tachima.*
Close your eyes.	*Nunkama.*
Turn off the light.	*Pulko.*

IN THE BEDROOM

Is this your first time?	*Chomuro hanunkoya?*
Tell me the truth.	*Sashil tero mal-hecho.*

I'm still a virgin.	*Na achikto chonyo ya.* (women) *Na achikto chongak iya.* (men)
I'm frightened.	*Muso-wo.*
Don't worry.	*Kokchong hachima.*
I'll be careful.	*Choshim halke.*
I wanna hold your hand.	*No sonchaba pogoshipo.*
Look into my eyes.	*Ne-nun chotaba.*
Hug me.	*Gyo anacho.*
Take your _____ off!	*_____ poso!*
clothes	*Ot*
jeans	*Chongpachi*
dress	*Turesu*
socks	*Yangmal*
sneakers	*Shinpal*

shoes	*Kudu*
bra	*Puracha*
underwear	*Penti**

* The Korean word *penti,* despite its derivation from the English "panty," is gender-neutral.

I'm cold!	*Na chuwo!*
	Chuwo!
Make me warm.	*Na tadutage hecho.*
Come closer to me.	*Nante to kakaiwa.*
That tickles.	*Kanchiro.*

IN BED

I wanna see your _____.	*Na ni _____ pogoshipo.*
I wanna touch your _____.	*Na ni _____ manchigoshipo.*
I wanna suck your _____.	*Na ni _____ balgoshipo.*
thing	*ko*
breasts	*chot*
pussy	*pochi*
dick	*chachi*
balls	*pural*
nipples	*chot-kokchi*
butt	*ongdong-i*
knees	*murup*
toes	*palkara*
shoes	*kudu*

I'm afraid I'll get pregnant.	*Imshin halkaba muso-wo.*
Use a condom!	*Kondom so!*
I don't like to wear a condom.	*Kondom sunungo shiro.*
If you don't wear a condom, I won't do it!	*Kondom ansumyon, anhalkoya!*
Oh, it feels so good!	*Ah, kibun choa!*
Touch me!	*Na manchocho!*
Bite me!	*Kemurocho!*
More, more!	*To, to!*
Deeper, deeper!	*To kipsuki!*
Faster, faster!	*Topali, topali!*

Wait, wait!   *Kidalyo, kidalyo!*

I'm coming, I'm coming!   *Sonda, sonda!**

> * Literally, "I'm shooting, I'm shooting!"

I came.   *Sata.*

I know.   *Ara.*

Did it feel good?   *Kibun choatso?*

Let's get married.   *Uri kyolhon hacha.*

I wanna be your wife.   *No-e puini tegoshipo.*

I wanna be your husband.   *No-e nampyoni tegoshipo.*

I don't wanna get married yet.	*Na chigum kyolhon hago shipchi ana.* *Na chigum kyolhon hagi shiro.*
I'm too young.	*Chigumun nomu il-lo.**

* Literally, "It's too early."

I'm already married.	*Na polso changa gatso.* *Na polso shichip gatso.*

I love you, but I can't become your (wife) (husband).	*Nul sarang-he, hachiman no-e (puini) (nampyoni) telsu opso.*
I need time to think.	*Sengakal shigani piryo-he.*
This is so sudden.	*Nomu kapchag iya.*

We must think about this.	*Uri to sengak-he paya telkot kate.*
Wanna come to _____ with me?	*Narang kachi _____ kale?*
the US	*miguk*
Canada	*kenada*
Europe	*yurop*
Taiwan	*taeman*
I wanna stay in Korea.	*Na hanguk-e ikoshipo.*

LEVING

Let's not see each other again.	*Uri tashinun manachi malcha.*
I hate you!	*No shiro!* *Miwo!*
Don't call me again.	*Tashin chonwa hachima.*
Get lost!	*Kocho!*

Give it up, already.	*Toisang noryok hachima.*
I don't love you anymore.	*Nol ichen sarang-hachi ana.*
You're boring.	*No chemi opso.**

* Literally, "You are no fun."

Stop following me.	*Na kuman chocha tanyo.*
Do you have another lover?	*Na malgo tarun sarami itso?*
It's my fault.	*Nega chalmot hetso.*
Can we start again?	*Tashi shichak halsun opso?*
I can't live without you.	*No opshi salsun opso.*
Please understand me.	*Chebal nachom i-he hecho.*
I'll never forget you.	*Nol ichulsu opsulkoya.*
Can we still be friends?	*Uri chinguro chinelsu itso?*

I will always love you.	*Nol onchena sarang-halkoya.*
I'll miss you.	*Pogoshipo chilkoya.*
I'll always think about you.	*Onchena nosengak halke.*
I'll call you from New York.	*Nyu yok eso chonwa halke.*
I'll call you when I come back.	*Torawaso chonwa halke.*
I'll be back soon.	*Na kot olke.*
Do you have to go?	*Kok kayade?*
Please don't go!	*Chebal kachima!*
Stay here with me.	*Narang yogi kachi itso cho.*
I have to go.	*Na kayade.*
Try to understand.	*Ihe hecho.*
Take care of your health.	*Momchori chal-he.*
Don't cry!	*Ulchima!*

Wipe your tears!   *Nunmul taka!*

Wait for me.   *Nal kidalyo cho.*

OTHER TITLES IN THE
YENBOOKS LIBRARY

Business Guide to Japan
by Boye L. DeMente
Everything you need to know to win at the business game in Japan is explained in this no-nonsense guide. Learn how to penetrate company bureaucracy, read subtle signs to come out ahead on the negotiating table, and master the art of after-hours business with this guide to doing business in Japan. All the practical tips and hints you'll need to be a success.

The Completely Non-Authoritative Guide to Japan
by Paul Nowak and Robert Urowsky
A zany, comically illustrated portrayal of Japan that is right on the mark! Page after page of hilarious cartoons lampoons the Japanese and Japan's foreign community. This lively guide takes the who, the what, and the *why* out of living in Japan. Though not the most erudite guide, it might be the funniest!

"Is That 'L' as in Rome?" "No, It's 'R' as in London.": Gems of Japanized English
by Miranda Kenrick
This book of absurd Japanese uses and abuses of English is sure to tickle your funny bone. Longtime Japan resident Miranda Kenrick offers a humorous but affectionate take on Japan, and her compilation adds up to a thoroughly enjoyable portrait of that country's lighter side.

Japanese Slang Uncensored
by Peter Constantine
Japanese Slang Uncensored pulls no punches in drawing a detailed picture of the richness of Japanese slang. It features the earthy and colorful patois of *yakuza*, trendy club-goers, bad boys, working girls, and other such characters. Constantine skillfully traces the fascinating origin of the expressions and shows how and where they are used.

Japan's Sex Trade
by Peter Constantine
Japan's Sex Trade offers a probing, step-by-step tour of the astonishing professional sex scene in Japan: love hotels, soaplands, S&M snack bars, and kinky salons. The highlight of each section is a listing of the language of these "floating worlds," with their service menus explained in detail. Scandalous and controversial, this book will fascinate the reader.

Lover's Guide to Japan
by Boye L. De Mente
Whether you're a newcomer to Japan or an old hand, this guide can be your ticket to after-hours fun. Where to go, what to do, what to say—it's all here. *Lover's Guide to Japan* gives you instant access to all the (sensual) mysteries of Japan and the Japanese. Find out where the action is and how to get some!

Making Out in Chinese
by Ray Daniels
This Chinese version of the hugely successful *Making Out in Japanese* lets you skip the grammar lesson and go straight to the everyday language of the people. All the necessary words and phrases for drinking, socializing, fighting, and romancing are included in clear, easy-to-understand romanization.

Making Out in Indonesian
by Peter Constantine
At long last—a guidebook to Indonesian slang as Indonesians really speak it. Even those who speak no Indonesian at all can quickly learn hundreds of colorful, colloquial expressions to make friends, talk about food, converse with taxi drivers, and much more. All Indonesian phrases are given in simple romanization.

Making Out in Japanese
by Todd and Erika Geers
From the language used between friends to easy conversation in a bar, this best-selling book provides you with all the common words

and phrases used in casual Japanese. Accompanied by a pronunciation guide and a key to male/female usage, this book will bring you to a new level of fluency and communication in Japanese.

More Making Out in Japanese
by Todd and Erika Geers

This book offers you even more handy Japanese phrases to start up a romance, handle bilingual marriage and children, and more. Filled with lovers' language and fighting words, this book will add zest to your social life and help you along the sometimes rocky road to romance in Japan.

Making Out in Thai
by John Clewley

Making Out in Thai is the latest addition to our popular *Making Out* series. This book, written by a native English speaker who also speaks Thai, enables even readers who speak no Thai to make new friends, order meals, argue with taxi drivers, woo sweethearts, and more. Simple romanization provided for all Thai phrases.

Murder at the Tokyo American Club
by Robert J. Collins

Welcome to the Tokyo American Club, where club manager Pete Peterson's head has just been found bobbing in the swimming pool. A headless torso was found alongside it, but the body doesn't match the head. A swelling list of suspects is investigated as the police chief pieces together the puzzle, as well as the body parts. Comic intrigue unfolds as the private lives of club members are revealed.

Outrageous Japanese: Slang, Curses, and Epithets
by Jack Seward

Yes, Japanese people do swear—and so can you with this book! It covers threats, taunts, curses, sex, booze, money, and more. Fun and instructive, this book is perfect for students of all levels, as well as readers simply interested in Japan. Author Seward has been involved with the Japanese language as a student, teacher, and author for more than 25 years and will help you speak your mind—outrageously!

Tokyo Pink Guide
by Steven Langhorne Clemens
The first book to tell foreign men and women how to enter the doors of Japan's "anything goes" pleasure palaces. Learn what to expect at and beyond the front door and get tips on what to wear, dos and don'ts, and prices.

The Truth About Japan
selected and edited by Andrew Watt
This hilarious collection contains over 300 excerpts on the people, entertainment, and social customs of old Japan by a motley collection of foreigners. Find out what it was really like before the world learned about sushi.

Using Japanese Slang
by Anne Kasschau and Susumu Eguchi
Japanese grammar texts a little dry sometimes? *Using Japanese Slang* takes you on a tour of the living language, not only introducing colloquialisms, but also their origins and the people who use them. Let this book put some color into your Japanese language experience.

Winning Pachinko: The Game of Japanese Pinball
by Eric C. Sedensky
Pachinko, Japan's biggest form of gambling, is played by over 30 million Japanese in smoke-choked parlors of mind-rattling noise and glaring lights. In *Winning Pachinko*, author Sedensky opens the parlor door to the English-speaking world and guides readers through the essentials of playing for fun—and profit.

Women of the Orient
by Boye L. De Mente
Enjoy a whirlwind tour of Asia's exotic cities and discover the special character and charms of some of the world's most feminine women. This unique book gives fascinating and titillating descriptions of the most exotic women in the world from Japan, Korea, Vietnam, China, Thailand, and the Philippines.

ABOUT THE AUTHOR

Born in London and brought up in Austria and Greece, Peter Constantine writes fiction and translates literature from Afrikaans, German, Greek, Dutch, Portuguese, Spanish, and Italian. He is the author of *Japanese Street Slang, Japan's Sex Trade, Japanese Slang Uncensored,* and *Making Out in Indonesian.*